SPEAK
INSIDE
THE BOX

ON-SCREEN PRESENTATION TIPS FOR SPEAKERS, TRAINERS, AND LEADERS

DAVE BRICKER

Speak Inside the Box

ESSENTIAL ABSURDITIES PRESS

Copyright 2020 Essential Absurdities Press
Book design and production by Dave Bricker

With gratitude to Libby Kiszner, Bud Maddock, and
Dr. Margarita Gurri for fast-turnaround editing, and friendship

ISBN: 978-0-9862960-6-2

"If you want to be a better photographer, stand in front of more interesting stuff."

— Jim Richardson

Contents

SPEAK INSIDE THE BOX

ON-SCREEN PRESENTATION TIPS FOR SPEAKERS, TRAINERS, AND LEADERS

DAVE BRICKER

Introduction

The coronavirus hit. *Boom!* Employees were sent home to work remotely. Some were sent home to not work at all. Conferences, conventions, and speaking engagements were canceled—all of them!

Whether or not these conditions prevail as you read this, "virtual" presentation skills have forever increased in value. Mastering your laptop's built-in webcam and learning how to use videoconferencing software is cost of entry. Leaders, speakers, trainers, and other presenters must acquire new skills and deliver a "big stage" experience on-screen—speaking "inside the box."

This book will help you thrive in this new world.

- Understand and leverage the differences between face-to-face and on-screen presentation

- Adapt traditional speaking skills to on-screen speaking

- Develop new presentation skills that set you apart

- Practice a success mindset that focuses on new, exciting opportunities rather than on old, lost ones

- Acquire the tools and gear you need to look and sound great on-screen

- Become a "virtualoso" presenter!

Presentation skills will always be the foundations of leadership, confidence, clarity, credibility, and opportunity. Leaders catalyze the building of communities—which are ever more important when people interact from remote locations.

Speak Inside the Box covers the technology, equipment, and know-how required to connect and engage from the virtual stage, though it does not recommend specific equipment or software. The worlds of technology and video production are both evolving rapidly. View YouTube tutorials and read product reviews carefully to educate yourself on *today's* best tools and practices.

The guidance in this book will help you "dress for success" at online meetings, reconfigure your speaking and presentation skills, and deliver a "big stage" experience from a home studio. If you're a leader, speaker, trainer, or professional who relies on personal connection and professional standards, this book offers the support you need to make your message engage viewers who are not in the room with you.

1. Speak Inside the Box

I*'ve been videoconferencing for years; this will be easy!* I thought as I began my first virtual speech. When it was over, I was surprised at my lackluster performance, and by the number of filler words I used—ums, ers, and ahs—speaking habits I had worked to banish from my presentations a long time ago.

What just happened?

Because I had been "videoconferencing for years," I slipped into "conversation mode." I sat in my chair in front of my webcam and instead of delivering a dynamic speech, I gave a well-organized lecture. *Boring!*

Conversation is natural, informal, and easy to engage in from a sitting position. But try speaking dynamically from a chair and you'll understand where this book's title came from. Fitting a speech into a head-and-shoulders-sized video "box" is awkward and diminishing. Sitting compresses the diaphragm and interferes with vocal projection. Some newscasters and other broadcast performers do learn to perform effectively while seated—and there is much to be learned from watching them—but broadcasters rarely employ the same range of volume, intensity, and pitch that professional speakers do. When performance dynamics exceed the size of the performance area, most speakers "shrink to fit."

Public speaking is usually performed by a presenter who stands. Stage positioning "anchors" characters, ideas, and points in the timeline of the narrative. Hand and body gestures create emphasis. Adapting these stage skills to the virtual world is one of the challenges addressed by this book.

If you want to participate in casual meetings and discussions, your built-in webcam and microphone will do the job. If you want to look polished and professional on-screen, this equipment will not be sufficient.

To become a "virtualoso" speaker, you'll need a bigger stage — actual or virtual. The "talking head" approach is not conducive to effective on-screen presentations. The popular but erroneous question of "How can I deliver my speech through a webcam?" is analogous to "How can I eat my steak through a straw?"

If you're a professional trainer, speaker, leader, or other presenter, you need a professional videoconferencing set-up for meetings and discussions, *and* a separate set-up for presentation and performance.

DAVE BRICKER

Speaking Styles

Differences between presentations, meetings, and training sessions inform effective approaches to virtual speaking. The following loose categories of professional interaction and their respective requirements provide a backbone for the advice offered in this book.

- **Meetings** involve a *group* of people engaged in discussion. Each has an opportunity to speak—to become a presenter—within the larger conversation, though there may or may not be an official group leader or main presenter.

- **Presentations** typically involve a speaker who works in a presentation area—a "stage." This can be an actual stage or just the front of a conference room. Those in the room assume the roles of "presenter" and "audience."

- **Training sessions** usually feature a central presenter, but they involve discussion, live-coaching, and other forms of audience participation. Training is a much more interactive process than presentation.

These distinctions and the significant gray areas where they overlap are simple and intuitive. Think about how each format (or combination of them) requires different techniques, technologies, and mindsets.

Each presentation type implies a different social hierarchy within the "event culture." If you're a team-member participating in a virtual town-hall meeting where the company is seeking input from the employees, upstaging the boss with a fancy virtual event stage is a bad idea. If you're a professional speaker giving a video keynote address at a virtual conference, delivering it via your laptop's built-in webcam will underwhelm your audience and the meeting organizers who hired you. Trainers and educators must establish authority and credibility, yet be accessible and approachable to trainees. A "rock star" virtual stage will not build the kind of rapport that invites open discussion and participation.

What types of virtual presentations are you most likely to deliver? Are you a teacher? A keynote speaker? A team leader? Or do you speak in different ways to different audiences at different times? Do you present at meetings and also participate in discussions?

A webcam and microphone may be all you need. Or you may want to build a physical stage in your basement with lights and cameras and a control room for your engineers and video editing staff. Most presenters will do best with something in-between. How can you best serve your audience? Do you want to look "casual-professional" or convince viewers that you're a celebrity? Choose your technology and develop a presentation style that suits your audience, your objectives, and your budget.

The chapters ahead offer guidance on what approaches to adopt and how to use them effectively.

2. Technical Set-up

Look Better; Sound Better

Desktop video is the entry point for most virtual speakers. Built-in cameras and microphones have been standard features in laptops, tablets, and phones for well over a decade. Most people capable of using a computer have a working familiarity with videoconferencing.

Because most devices offer "pretty good" audio and video quality, and because "pretty good" serves the needs of most people, professionals stand out by upgrading their cameras and microphones to "excellent."

New technology is introduced every day. Specific recommendations are avoided in favor of spelling out the pros and cons of various choices. Research today's offerings and understand your options before purchasing new equipment. This chapter offers an overview of the on-board equipment you probably already have, and options for improving it.

Bandwidth

Crisp images and sparkling audio consume *a lot* of bandwidth. If your Internet connection is slow, a high-end camera and microphone won't deliver noticeable results.

When possible, avoid wireless (wi-fi) connections in favor of cabling your computer directly into the Internet. The advantages of a "wired" connection are higher speed and greater reliability. Professional presenters ensure that any bandwidth bottlenecks occur *after* their video messages have left their studios.

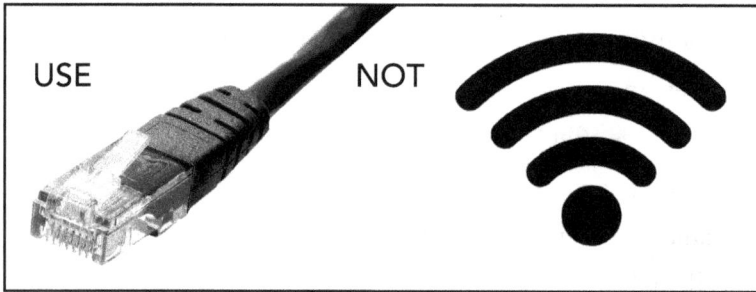

Ask your Internet provider about high-speed service plans. For HD video, you'll need at least 1.2 Mbps (Megabits per second). With 4K video emerging as a new standard, higher speeds are required. Fortunately, 20Mbps and higher service plans are common and affordable. If you're speaking from home, you might be presenting at the same time that others in your household are streaming movies or playing online games. Invest in the bandwidth you need to keep those megabits flowing.

Processor Speed

Because video is captured, compressed, and broadcasted in real time, videoconferencing places significant demands on your computer's processor. If your computer is relatively new, you probably have the requisite processing power to stream high quality video. If upgrading to a higher resolution camera, read the specifications to ensure your machine can handle the additional video loads.

Webcams

The webcam built into your laptop, tablet, or phone has a tiny lens and limited features. Upgrading to a better camera offers several advantages:

- A bigger lens and higher quality optics deliver sharper images and better color.

- Many cameras come with software that automatically enhances images when the subject is backlit (for example, sitting in front of a bright, open window), or when the light is lower than optimal.

- Some webcam software applications allow you to adjust a variety of variables including focus, color correction, depth of field, and magnification.

- Some newer webcams allow you to broadcast in 4K[1] — at four times the resolution of standard HD (1080p) Video. Watch for this to slowly become the new standard.

- Many webcams come with built-in microphones that are of higher quality than the built-in variety. If you're traveling with a laptop, clipping a quality webcam/microphone combination to the top of your screen will provide a better experience than off-the-shelf versions.

Use a webcam for meetings and conversations when you are seated close to the camera. For keynotes, training, and important presentations, use the "big stage" solutions discussed later in this book.

Lights and Lighting

Join an online meeting and observe the differences between the appearance of the participants' video streams. Mary is speaking in front of a bright window; all you can see of her is the outline of her head. Bill has the shades drawn; his image is dark and yellow, and few details are visible. Shari has a bright desk light shining down on her; the "hot spots" on her cheeks and forehead are dazzling. The twin wall lamps behind Eddie look like "electric

1. The merits of 4K video are discussed later.

A professional webcam offers a bigger, better lens than built-in models.

antlers" sticking out of his head." Good lighting is a matter of experimentation, trial, and error, but a few simple principles can guide your choices:

- Bright lights behind you from lamps and windows create "backlighting." Your camera will respond by dimming the scene, much as you would squint if staring into a spotlight.

The subject ends up displayed as a dark silhouette against a white background.

- Illuminate what you want the camera to see. Close shades and drapes or speak with a wall behind you.

- Bright lights in your face are uncomfortable to look at, and they create "hot spots" on the video. Dim or insufficient lighting won't bring out the contrast and details you want to show in your video.

- Consider using several LED panel lights with diffusion screens—sheets of white plastic in front of the LED array. Mount these lights on tripods or on the wall behind your work station. Using more lights of lower intensity enables you to create a sharp, colorful image without blinding yourself. A pair of quality lights with stands can be purchased for under $200.

Good lighting is often overlooked or put off "until later," but it makes a huge difference in the quality of your

LED panel

on-screen presentation. If forced to choose between purchasing lights or a new webcam, buy the lights.

Microphones

Microphones are your listeners' ears. Though high-end recording studio microphones can cost five figures, a minor upgrade goes a long way for those who wish to improve the experience delivered by their presentations.

Because most people tend to be more visual than auditory, your on-board microphone (or the slightly better one in your new web-cam) will work for basic videoconferencing. As long as you can be heard without distortion (which is usually more a function of your Internet speed and audio settings than of the quality of your microphone), enjoy the blessings of your convenient, tiny,

In this image of online meeting participants, which ones are backlit, too brightly lit (hot spots), not lit well enough (minimal range from shadows to highlights), or show background clutter?

and cable-free built-in mic while you are seated at your computer. If you want to bump up the quality and filter out more ambient sound, consider a higher-end option.

Studio condenser microphones are preferred by podcasters and broadcasters. These mics are typically mounted on a retractable arm with a shock/vibration reducing elastic suspension. A range of options is available from $30–$50 with high-er-end models costing more. Some are equipped with USB connections that al-low you to plug them directly into your computer. Most use a standard (XLR) microphone cable, and require an au-dio interface ($50–$200) that converts the microphone signal to USB. Though this might seem unnecessary, a separate audio interface brings additional advantages that will be discussed later in this book. Advantages and disadvantages:

Studio Condensor Mic

- High-quality sound is best for audio-centric presentations

- Most studio condenser mics are powered by your system so they're not battery-dependent.

- Large size adds clutter to your video presentation

- Thick cables and large microphone add physical clutter to your desktop/work area

Lavalier and headset microphones work well on stage, and they work well for most types of presentations. An advantage of these microphones is that they're attached to you. Moving closer or farther away from your camera won't change the volume or clarity of the sound. Clip a lavalier (lav) mic to your collar and start moving. Untethering the microphone from the computer is the first step in gaining the mobility you need to become a more effective on-screen presenter.

Lavalier mics are available in both wired and wireless models. Most feature a clip-on microphone that's connected by a cable run inside the speaker's clothing to a small "bodypack." This device transmits the signal wirelessly or via a microphone cable to your computer's audio input. Headset microphones are configured in a similar fashion. Advantages and disadvantages:

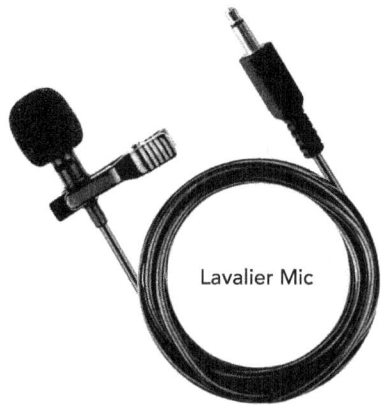

Lavalier Mic

- Better mobility means freedom to focus on stagecraft

Bluetooth Mic

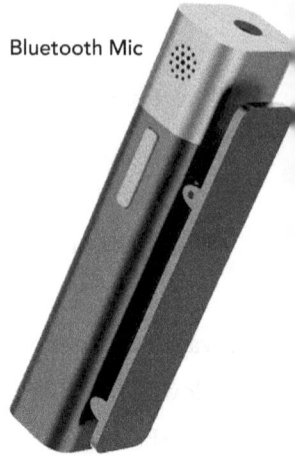

- Light, portable, and unobtrusive

- Excellent sound quality

- Almost invisible when presenting

- Affordable ($40–$500+)

- Wireless options reduce "cable clutter" but introduce greater risk of hum, interference, distortion, or other glitches.

- Most lav/headset gear is dependent on small batteries (AA or AAA) to operate properly. Keep spares on-hand and always replace batteries in advance of an important presentation.

Bluetooth microphones are a relative newcomer to the presentation game. Charge up the on-board battery, tether to your phone or computer, clip the microphone to your lapel, and start speaking.

Advantages and disadvantages:

- No cables! No bodypacks or wires inside your clothing!

- Works at distances up to 65 feet

- Battery-dependent so watch your charge level

- Bluetooth is prone to interference and speed drops

As you consider enhancing your built-in camera and microphone, read online reviews carefully. New equipment is constantly introduced; today's must-have technology may be forgotten tomorrow.

Cables are more reliable than wireless connections, but they add clutter to your work area. Choose cables of the appropriate length. For example, if your condenser mic sits in front of your computer, a three- or four-foot cable will eat less space than a twenty-foot coil wrapped up in twist-ties. And all cables are not created equal. Invest in quality cabling to reduce noise and increase longevity.

Understand how our microphone will connect to your computer. USB and standard 1/8-inch audio connectors can plug into your USB port or microphone jack. Bluetooth microphones will synch wirelessly with your device. A microphone with a standard XLR plug will require a converter or USB audio interface.

USB

1/8" Microphone

Before you move on to create a virtual performance space, familiarize yourself with the capabilities of your new equipment. Open a one-person meeting—just you–

XLR Microphone

and observe yourself. Adjust your camera and lighting. Experiment with your microphone(s).

Try an informal videochat with friends. Compare the appearance of your screen to other online meeting participants. Listen to the quality of their audio.

The set-up and performance tips introduced in the following chapter will make you a better on-screen speaker. You'll rely on these same skills later when you graduate from videoconferencing to virtual speaking.

3. The Virtual Conference Table

Optimize Your Presentation Space

Many presentation compromises are caused by computers that provide a camera, microphone, screen, keyboard, and speakers in one compact package. If there ever was a "marriage of convenience," this is it. Marvelous as this may be, when you wish to go beyond casual conversation to professional presentation, you'll find that good camera position becomes bad keyboard position. When we're the perfect distance from the camera, we may be too far from the keyboard or mouse, and the microphone may pick up more background noise.

Aside from better quality sound and video, an added microphone and webcam offer opportunities to physically uncouple important presentation tools. Much of this chapter discusses how to separate your microphone, screen, keyboard, and speakers. Optimize your presentation space by placing each component in its ideal position.

Create an attractive, ergonomic, and efficient presentation space. You'll look better, sound better, and feel more comfort-

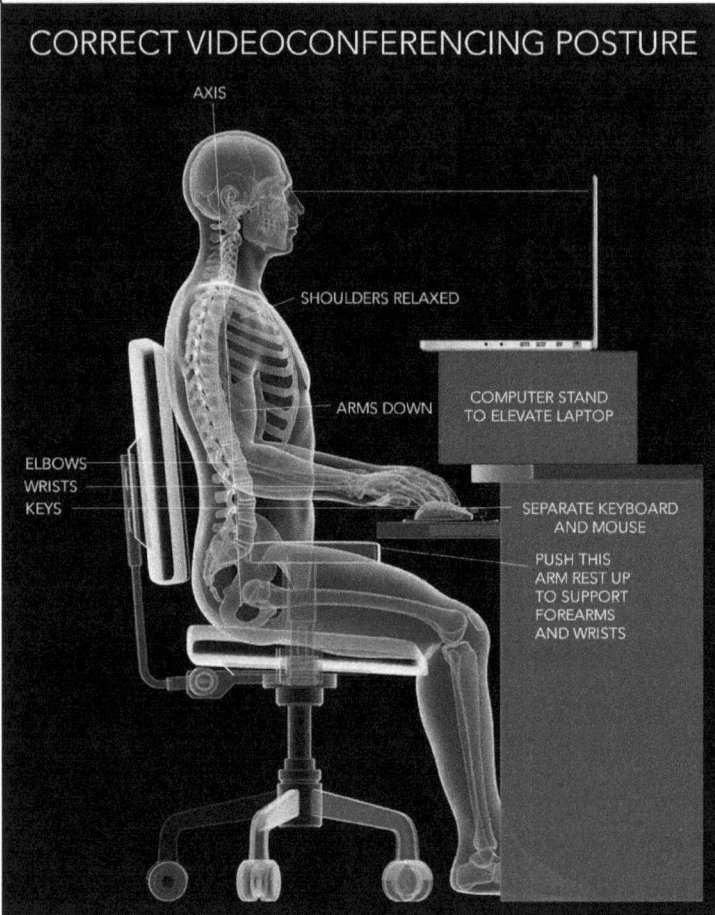

CORRECT VIDEOCONFERENCING POSTURE

AXIS

SHOULDERS RELAXED

ARMS DOWN

COMPUTER STAND
TO ELEVATE LAPTOP

ELBOWS
WRISTS
KEYS

SEPARATE KEYBOARD
AND MOUSE

PUSH THIS
ARM REST UP
TO SUPPORT
FOREARMS
AND WRISTS

able as you work, meet with others, and demonstrate leadership on the screen.

Backgrounds

Lights…! Camera…! Hold on … you're not quite ready. Backgrounds are discussed in this section because unlike your microphone and webcam, they are a part of your presentation that viewers can see. Meeting participants may not notice your clear image and crisp audio—after all, that's how you're supposed to sound and look—but they will notice your contribution to the virtual conference room.

The Elephant in the Room

Your webcam offers other meeting participants a clear view of your study, garage, bedroom, living room, garden shed—wherever it is that you're broadcasting from. This may be fine for casual conversation,

Background clutter

but professionals know that backgrounds are the new frontier in professional fashion. It doesn't matter whether you're even dressed from the waist down—nobody will see—but the environment you work in/from says much about your professional standards. Even if you're working at home, show them you're at work.

Create a "personality wall." In my presentation work, I speak about business story-telling using a nautical model I call StorySailing.® The shelves

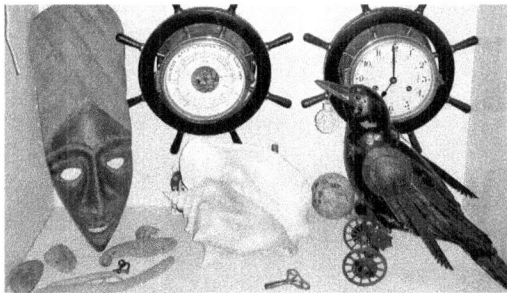

Personality wall

behind my desk hold a selection of nautical gear—a sextant, binoculars, seashells, and miscellaneous maritime items—along with books I've written, edited, or designed. My guitar hangs on the wall beside the bookshelf. The display offers books and conversation starters that are relevant to my interests and the services I offer.

I use my bookshelf as a background when meeting one-on-one with friends and clients; it's casual and personal, but professional. When attending group meetings or presenting, I use a digital background that's free of clutter and distraction.

Whether your background is a white wall, a favorite piece of artwork, or a shelf full of bric-a-brac, make it relevant to what you do personally and professionally. Your bed, your living room couch, and your partially open bathroom door add no value to your professional communications. If it's visible on-screen, it should make a meaningful contribution to your appearance or message.

Green Screens

A popular alternative to showing off the bedroom vanity is to use a green screen, also called a chromakey screen. Hang the screen behind you, close enough so the edges aren't visible through the camera. Most online meeting applications allow you to choose an image as a background. The software magically substitutes your background image for any of the green areas.

Desk with green screen

Any solid color will work … as long as you don't wear anything of a similar hue. I learned this the hard way when I hung up a dark blue blanket, specified that as my chromakey color, and wore a medium blue shirt. All was well until I moved away from my lights. The software lost its ability to discern the difference

The "invisible shirt."

between the blue shirt and the blue background, and this rendered my shirt transparent. The background image showed where my torso was supposed to be, revealing only my disconnected arms and head. I moved forward and back, trying to find the right proximity to the camera while staying close enough so my shirt remained visible. My shirt flickered in and out, alternating with the background.

As long as it's not Saint Patrick's Day, a bright green purpose-made green screen is unlikely to clash with your wardrobe colors. If green is your signature color, use a blue screen instead. Meeting software makes chromakey screens easy to use. Open the settings panel for your meeting software, select the "green screen" option, and specify a background image. Just be mindful of color choices when dressing for meetings and presentations; that jade necklace may appear as a hole in your chest.

How to use a green screen properly is worthy of a book in itself. Watch a few of the many YouTube tutorials posted by professional videographers to optimize your results.

Some general principles:

- The green screen should be as free from wrinkles and fold lines as possible. Sags and wrinkles create shadows that effectively change the color of the green screen where they occur. This results in areas of partial transparency and strange artifacts in the video.

Wrinkled or unevenly lit screens cause artifacts in the video background.

- The farther you are from the green screen, the less likely you are to cast shadows on it. Like wrinkles, shadows also cause dark areas on the screen that make it more difficult for the software to make good decisions about what parts of the image to make transparent, especially around fine details like hair.

Shadows on the screen can cause problems with chromakey backgrounds.

- If you have trouble getting good results, place separate lights behind you for the green screen to keep it evenly lit and less prone to shadowing.

Note the separate lights for the green screen and the speaker

Select a Background Image

Though it may be tempting to select a colorful picture of autumn leaves, a mountain stream, or a rainbow for a background, the most important element in the video frame is you. Resist the urge to decorate. Your video background is not your private computer desktop. Choose a simple, elegant backdrop that keeps viewers' focus on your face and your message.

Background images belong to one of two styles:

The self-contained background image creates the equivalent of a PowerPoint slide where your video feed is the content. Add a logo, your name, contact information, or other branding near the top or sides. Make the background a solid color, a subtle gradient, or an interesting

A distracting background image

texture (wood grain, paper, canvas, etc.) of medium brightness and intensity. A simple background can be elegant and classy, and it won't compete with you for viewers' attention.

"Window-into-a-larger world" background images show a glimpse of something much larger than the screen. Imagine you wanted to use a fish tank as a video background. If the tank were the same size as your screen, the fish would swim up to the edges and turn around. If the tank were much larger

A simple self-contained background image keeps viewers' focus on you.

than the camera view, fish would swim in one side and out the other, suggesting that you have an entire ocean behind you. A cloudy sky would work the same way. Show a small piece of a big stage, conference room, or appropriate venue to suggest you're in a "bigger" place, even if you're in a tiny studio. The background image for my own "virtual stage"[2] shows the bottom of a giant LED screen behind me, suggesting that I'm standing on a giant event stage in a conference meeting hall.

In the example on the left, the fish can't swim beyond the screen. On the right, they have an entire ocean to roam in.

I used a video background example—the fish tank—to make a point in the previous paragraph, but unless you intend to use something subtle—like a video loop of very slowly changing background colors—resist the temptation to add a gigantic moving distraction to your on-screen appearance.

Virtual Backgrounds

Some meeting software allows you to create a "virtual" back-

2. See page 65

ground without using a green screen. The software analyzes the video, makes a good guess at what's you and what's background, and substitutes the selected image for the background as if you had a green screen. Though this may be fun to play with, the results are not nearly as accurate as with a real, physical green screen, especially in low light. Disappearing hands and other body parts, transparent reflections in eyeglasses, and other strange

Virtual backgrounds are unreliable. Use a green screen.
The hoped-for result is on the left. The actual result is on the right.

anomalies are common. Amuse yourself with the virtual back-grounds feature enough to satisfy your curiosity and then throw it on the pile of never-to-be-used cheap computer tricks along with the checkerboard PowerPoint transition.

A physical green screen is affordable and easy to roll up and stow when you're done with your conference. Collapsible "window shade" versions are available, and small chromakey screens can even be affixed to the back of your chair.

Find Your Signature Background

When executed properly, a digital background will add a note of professionalism to your online presentation. In combination with your upgraded webcam and a quality microphone, you'll be the "best-dressed" person at the meeting without appearing pretentious or self-absorbed.

Take your digital appearance seriously. Most professionals have a lot more money invested in their professional attire than they do in their digital presentation tools. In a world that's rapidly pivoting to virtual presentations, it's time to invest in digital fashion. In the virtual world, a sharp background is a powerful and easy way to dress for success.

Adjust Your Camera Position

Think about a recent, close, face-to-face discussion. Probably, you and your counterparts were all either sitting or standing. Eye contact is a powerful element of human connection so people position themselves at more or less equal heights when conversing. Your goal is to simulate this intimacy through the lens of your webcam.

Though few people make the mistake of positioning the webcam above eye level, a digital image is two-dimensional. A camera at top-of-head level will deliver a slightly squashed image of your face with more forehead visible than chin.

If the camera is too low, aside from looking up your nose, viewers will get a subconscious impression that you're looking down on them. A too-low camera is usually the result of a laptop sitting on a desk where the keyboard is accessible. The presenter folds the screen back far enough so the built-in webcam can see their face. This may be fine for casual conversation, but it's an amateurish approach to professional presentation.

If your laptop webcam is positioned where it should be at face level, this brings the keyboard to the top of your chest where it's difficult to see and use. How can you resolve this ergonomic dilemma?

Whether you use a purpose-built computer stand or a cardboard box, position your laptop's camera at eye level. Purchase a supplementary Bluetooth keyboard and mouse (~$20) for your physical desktop. This solution is simple and affordable, but 99% of laptop users won't think of it or bother. "Monkey trap" problems [3] like this offer easy advantages for those willing to make small adjustments.

Look your viewers straight in the eye by looking straight into the camera. They'll feel more like they're talking with you and less like they're talking to your technology.

---

3. The famous monkey trap places a bait inside a hole that's large enough for the monkey to reach in and grab. When his fist is closed around the prize, it's too big to pull back out. Refusing to let go, the monkey is trapped by his own small-mindedness.

Adjust Your Camera Distance

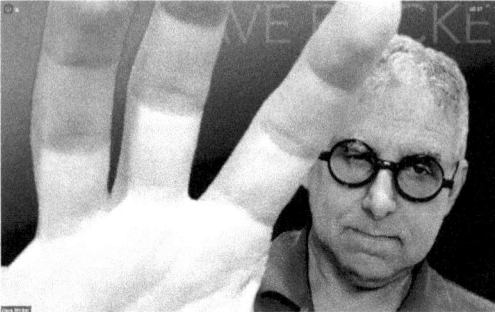

Moving hands close the camera creates extreme distortions of scale

Moving your face too close to the camera is *creepy.*

Most webcams offer a wide field of view. The upsides of this are that if you want to fit more of yourself in the video frame, you don't have to move very far from the camera. But because of the wide-angle lens, if you move a hand or finger closer to the camera, it becomes disproportionately huge. Give yourself room to lean toward the camera to show interest, but avoid close pointing and other gestures. You can keep your hands close to your body and still use them expressively.

Observe yourself in the webcam preview image.[4] Back away from the webcam until you like how and where you're positioned against the background. If you're too close, you'll look like a "peeping Tom." Don't crop off your chin or the top of your head. Leave some space above you. Show some shoulder.

4. Most computers have a preferences panel for selecting a video source. Use this preview video or open a session in your meeting application where you are the only participant.

Now try some more gestures. How big was that fish? Are your hands still in the frame? "Speaking inside the box" involves compromises. If you're like most people, you exaggerate when you describe your latest catch. Is there room in your frame to open your hands three feet apart and still keep them on-camera? That might actually be a more accurate way to describe that big one that got away.

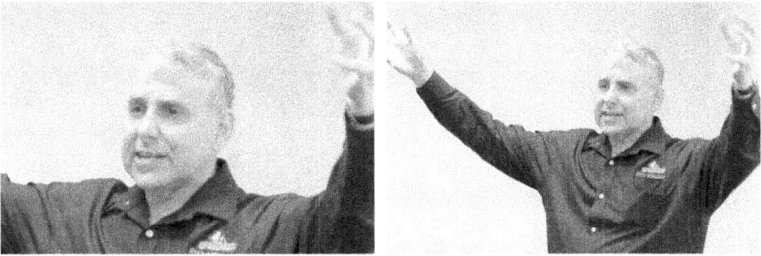

Move farther from the camera so you can use hand gestures effectively.

Experiment and find the "sweet spot" distance where you have room for hand gestures and you're far enough away to avoid distortions of proportion.

Adjust Your Lights

With your lights on, observe your preview video image. Turn the intensity up until you begin to see "hot spots"—areas of reflection, usually on cheeks or forehead—where the skin tones are replaced by white blotches. Back the intensity down until these disappear. This is where the diffusion screens on your lights help. A naked light bulb — a point of light — will cause bright reflections. Diffuse, filtered light is softer and less likely to cause hot spots. LED panels or studio "softbox" lights emit light from a large area rather than from a single point, which illuminates your face more naturally.

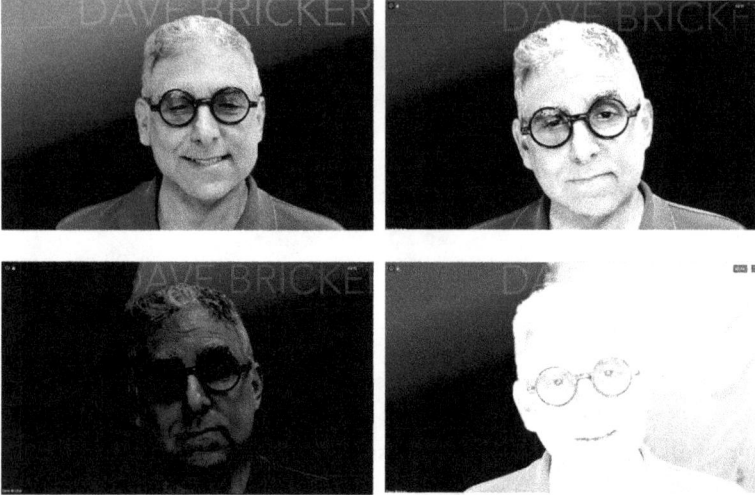

Upper left: correct exposure, Upper right: overexposed with "hot spots", Lower left: underexposed, Lower right: way overexposed

If your workplace has windows, your lighting requirements may vary depending on the time of day and how much sunlight is entering. Be mindful of the differences and adjust your lights accordingly. An alternative is to add additional ceiling or other off-camera room lights that can be turned on when the sun turns off. Don't drive yourself crazy chasing your light settings around the clock. Your upgraded webcam may have been bundled with software that does a good job adjusting the image automatically. Rather than getting lost in the woods of lighting and camera settings, ask yourself, "Does my video image look good?" Get comfortable and familiar enough with your camera and lighting equipment to make fast, easy, and intuitive adjustments as needed.

Choose Your Camera Settings

Is the color good? How about the contrast? Are the skin tones too red? Is the image too blue or too green? Use your webcam's software or a third-party application to adjust your camera settings until you're satisfied with the result. Usually, you can "set it and forget it." Get the adjustments right and then leave them be.

Set Your Microphone Level

Now that you and your camera are in position, adjust your microphone input level. If you're using the built-in microphone, you may have moved farther from the screen. Most computers offer an "automatic levels" option, but make sure you're being heard. In the sound preferences on your computer or in your meeting software, observe the sound meter as it responds to your voice.

Are you a dynamic speaker? Make sure your mic settings give you the range you need to get louder than the average conversation. Try a few loud sounds. An emphatic "Ho!" is conducive to vocal projection. Make sure louder sounds don't spike the meter or your listeners will hear distortion. Try a few softer passages. Do they register on the meter at all?

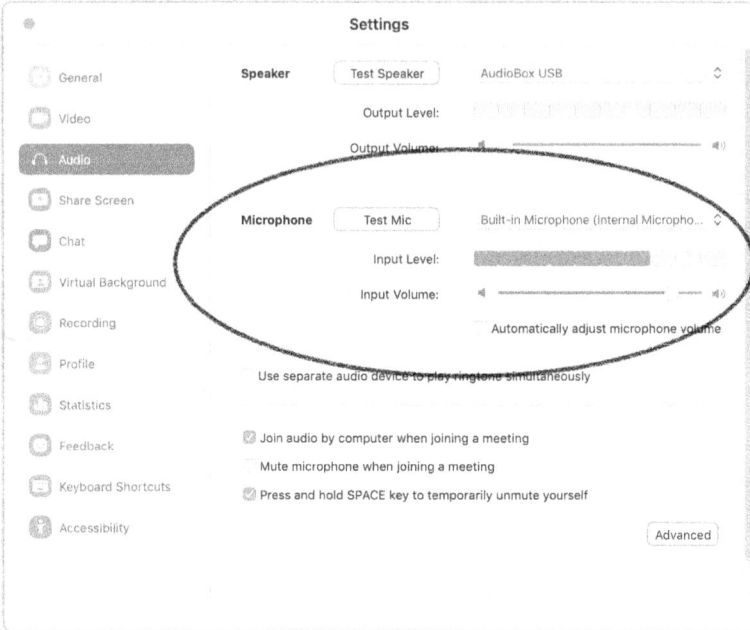

Set your microphone level in the settings/preferences panel of your meeting software.

If your meeting software allows, record yourself speaking at various levels of volume, pitch, and intensity. Is everything crisp and clear on playback? If not, adjust the levels and try again.

If you've moved away from the screen to fit in the frame, the placement of your microphone may now be less than ideal. Consider using a lavalier microphone on your collar or lapel that moves toward or away from the screen as you do.

A Note on Audio Speakers

Speakers — the kind that are part of your audio system, not the ones you clap for — aren't given much attention here because they're not part of your viewers' experience. As long as you can hear and understand other meeting participants, your built-in speakers may be all you need.

Most meeting and videoconferencing software offers built-in echo cancellation, but too much volume on your side may be picked up by your microphone. Turn your speaker volume down to fix these problems, or use a directional microphone that hears only what's in front of it.

Headphones are an effective solution for audio-only broadcasts, as they allow you to hear the discussion while the speakers are turned off; the microphone picks up only the pure sound of your voice. But on-screen, headphones detract from your appearance. For presentation work, adjust your speaker volume or use a directional microphone that gives you the freedom to hear the meeting without creating echoes or feedback. Wireless earbuds or in-ear headphones with tiny wires work if you can hide them behind your ears and under your hair.

Showtime!

Call a few friends. Set up an informal meeting. Tell your guests that you're making adjustments and upgrades so you can look and sound better on-screen. Ask for feedback. Compare the appearance of your video to theirs. If their experience is less than you hoped for, ask about their Internet speed and what equipment they're watching with. Not everyone will fully experience your "golden vision," but you'll find out what others see and get help making adjustments in your lights or webcam settings that improve the viewing experience for others.

4. Master the Online Meeting

Numerous applications compete for a share of the expanding virtual meetings market. To cover them in detail and explain their features and differences would fill too many pages and quickly render this book obsolete as new offerings are introduced.

This chapter explains features common to most online meetings and suggests ways you can use these tools as a leader or participant to enhance the meeting experience.

Look at the Camera

As natural as it may be to look into the eyes of the faces on your screen, the closest connection is made by looking directly into the camera. Though it may feel counterintuitive to look someone in the eyes by looking just above their eyes, addressing the camera is the best way to address the audience. Consider taping a small, colorful "look at the camera" reminder next to your webcam until the habit becomes natural.

Add a "Look Here!" sticker or even a pair of eyes to remind you to look into the camera.

Background Interference–
Pets, Kids, and Chatty Partners

You're working from home. Pretending otherwise is risky. Maintain as calm and quiet an atmosphere as possible, but manage interference with grace and dignity. Eventually, the dog will bark, the cat will sit on your keyboard, that package you've been waiting weeks for will finally arrive, your teenaged daughter will ask you for something she absolutely has to have right now, or your spouse will walk into your meeting space.

These intrusions are part of life. Post a sign on the door, alert family members that you'll be in a meeting, turn off the phone, and take other reasonable precautions, but don't let the inevitable disruption throw you off. When handled with gentle humor, pets, children, partners, and doorbells can add a personal touch to your meeting. I love working at home with my dogs. They make me smile and they make my clients smile, too.

Appoint a Meeting Manager

Online meetings can pack a lot of people into one virtual space. The most effective meetings are managed by one or more meeting hosts who watch for raised hands, check the chat window for comments and questions, and manage the mute settings for participants. If people who ask questions or raise hands are ignored, they will soon disengage. With proper management, guests will feel listened to and valued.

After a few meetings, especially with the same people in attendance, an effective online "meeting culture" will develop as participants and hosts become familiar and comfortable with whatever meeting platform is used.

As a leader, bear in mind that other participants, and the meeting host, may be less comfortable than you with technology and virtual gatherings. Offer gentle suggestions, not corrections. Show them how you do it rather than telling others to do it your way.

Send out a message in the group chat explaining that anyone who has questions is welcome to send you a private message. Helping colleagues without being a know-it-all is a hallmark of good leadership.

If the meeting host is new to managing online meetings, offer to co-host or help run the session. This alternative to "Let me show you how it's done" allows you to offer value while not making the meeting host look incompetent in front of other attendees.

Muting

Though pre-meeting chatter adds an element of informal congeniality, twenty cross-talking meeting participants won't get much work done.

Meeting hosts are given the ability to "mute all participants" when desired. Even if you're not the host, help create an online meeting culture where everyone learns to mute themselves when not speaking and remembers to unmute themselves when it's their turn.

Remember to mute yourself when you're not speaking.

Monitoring attendees' mute status is a chore that should be assigned to a host or co-host. Eventually, attendees will become accustomed to switching their mute buttons on and off as needed.

Audio and Video on/off

Many guests who are new to online meetings join a session and then have difficulty discovering how to turn on their audio and video. Ten participants begin issuing verbal instructions at the same time.

Create a meeting culture where a host or co-host takes on the role of looking for participants who need help. This functionary can hit the "mute all" button to stifle the chatter, reach out to support guests who need assistance, and then unmute everyone once the problems are solved.

Also helpful is to add simple directions to the emailed meeting invitation: "Sign into the meeting and then use the camera and microphone icons at the lower left of the meeting screen to activate your audio and video."

Recording Meetings

Various meeting platforms offer a variety of technical recording options. Discussion of recording here is confined to two areas:

Even if the screen says, "This Meeting is Being Recorded," offset liability and show respect by asking permission. Get a recorded, verbal assent. Explain what you intend to do with the recording. Some people want to speak "off the record," and if they wonder why you're capturing the session, they'll be less comfortable and less forthcoming with their conversation.

Speakers often shoot video of their on-stage performances. One of the best reasons to record a meeting is to revisit your presentation so you can make improvements. Tweak your lighting. Adjust your microphone. Don't wear a blue shirt with your blue background next time. Watch how key meeting attendees reacted. Did the audience laugh at your joke? In what other medium can you capture the simultaneous responses on the faces of a few dozen participants? Recordings of online presentations show both you and the audience — a feedback gold mine!

Gallery View Versus Speaker View

Those new to online meetings may be unfamiliar with the viewing options offered by most virtual meeting platforms.

Left: Speaker View, Right: Gallery View

In Speaker View, the software shows the screen of whomever is speaking at any given time. Usually, a selection of meeting attendee thumbnail images is displayed above the "big screen" of the speaker. This works well in small gatherings where people refrain from interruption. Speaker View keeps attendees focused on whomever is speaking, and it switches dynamically to follow the conversation.

The other option is Gallery View. This configuration displays as many meeting members as the software allows (~25) in rows and columns of video boxes. Whomever is speaking is highlighted with a colored outline, but all the faces remain equal-sized.

Gallery view is well-suited to online presentations because it gives speakers a view of multiple audience members. Given that everyone but you will probably have their microphone muted, you won't hear the laughter after your joke or the big, collective "oh" as the lightbulb turns on. Watching the faces of your audience gives you the important cues you need to be an engaging presenter.

Gallery view gives you excellent audience feedback.

Applause

Some meeting platforms offer an "applause" button that displays an illustration of a pair of clapping hands, but this is a weak substitute for the real thing. Real audiences offer a range of appreciative responses from "a sprinkle of applause" to "thunderous ovations."

Lightly clapping in front of your face while the mute button is on doesn't offer a sincere or enthusiastic response.

Remember those numbers they hold up during the Olympic games to rate the figure skaters and high divers? Consider developing a meeting culture where hand signals are used instead of clapping. Hold up one finger for "polite acknowledgement," two to recognize effort, three fingers for a "good performance," four for a "very good one," and five for an "excellent" one. Use two five-fingered hands for the rare, exceptional, "blow the doors off," life-changing presentation.

As a leader, your role is to innovate. Create meeting cultures where people can express themselves and interact authentically and naturally within the limitations of the meeting software.

Raise Your Hand

Though too many people interrupt when they want to speak, raising a hand has always been the polite way to ask for the floor. Meetings devolve into "competitive discussion" when the meeting facilitator refuses to manage the mayhem.

Gatherings are most effective when everyone feels listened to. When the topic changes before comments are heard, those with something to contribute feel excluded.

Whether you use your meeting software's "raise hand" button, ask to be recognized in the chat window, or physically raise your hand in front of your camera, it's up to a meeting host to pay attention and call on you.

Create a meeting culture where everyone knows what signal to use and someone is appointed to monitor "raised hand" requests.

The Chat Window

Use this straightforward little window to share questions and comments with the group and to send private messages to participants.

The chat window is an excellent place to share links. "I've just posted a link to a YouTube video in the chat. I'm going to mute everyone, give you three minutes to watch it, and then call you back to the session."

You can also post files if your meeting software allows. "Download and open the PDF I just posted in the chat. I'll give you a moment to look it over and then we'll talk about how to use it."

Because everyone has their eyes on the video feed, it's easy to overlook comments in the chat. Make sure a meeting host monitors the chat window and alerts attendees when important questions and comments are posted.

Breakout Rooms

Some meeting platforms offer virtual "breakout rooms" where sub-groups can engage in discussion before returning to the main session.

Use meeting rooms to sequester impromptu speech contest entrants before calling them back to the contest room to respond to the secret question or prompt.

For large meetings, remove small groups of random guests from the crowded meeting hall into separate rooms for light networking or discussion.

Create separate rooms for topical discussion. "Those wishing to talk about green screens, go to room A. Microphones are being discussed in room B. Learn more about digital backgrounds in Room C."

Meeting rooms are especially useful for trainers. If you're used to asking groups of people to work on an exercise for a short period and then report their results to the larger group, breakout rooms are an ideal solution. Read more on training strategies later in this book.

Innovate new ways to promote audience interaction with this underused feature, especially when working with large groups.

Polls

Meeting polls encourage interaction and audience engagement. The trick is to know they're there and set them up in advance of the meeting. Essentially, a meeting poll is a multiple-choice question. Give your meeting attendees an opportunity to click on a response and then share the answers.

Use meeting polls for ... well ... polls. If you need to vote on an issue, discover a priority, pick a winning contestant, or elect a leader, this simple tool will collect opinions and share the results.

Screen-sharing

The ability to share your screen in an online meeting offers a fantastic tool for engagement ... and a diabolical method for violating commonsense rules of tasteful presentation.

When screen-sharing is invoked, you'll be presented with an option to share the screen of any application running on your computer, your entire desktop (everything visible), any open window, or even a connected device like a phone or tablet. If you run numerous applications simultaneously, you may be offered a wide and confusing array of options.

Open a practice meeting in advance of the main session so you can quickly navigate to the appropriate window when it's your turn to share your screen. Also, though sharing your desktop may seem like an easy, one-size-fits-all solution, your viewers may end up seeing your private pop-up messages and other alerts. A reminder that "today is trash day" won't add much professionalism to your presentation.

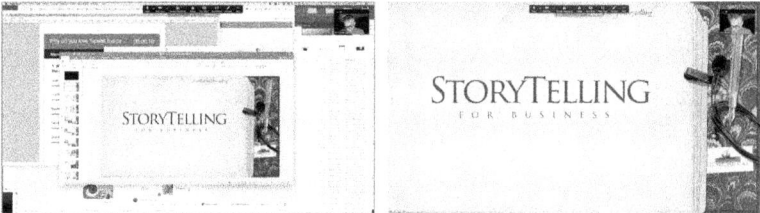

Left: Sharing the desktop is like showing off your cluttered bedroom.
Right: Share only the application your viewers need to see.

Avoid common mistakes made by PowerPoint presenters:

- Don't show large blocks of text, complex spreadsheets, or images you're not licensed to share.

- Don't post text and then read it to your audience.

- Don't add superfluous animations and transitions.

- Instead of sharing video content in your web browser, post a link and let attendees watch on their own systems. The smoothness of the video and the audio track will be much better.

PowerPoint

Because of its popularity with presenters, PowerPoint (and similar presentation software) deserves special mention. If you share a PowerPoint presentation, your video feed can be presented alongside it.

Unfortunately, if you want to view the presentation notes (presenter view) you'll need a second monitor. Though suitable monitors can be purchased inexpensively (~$120), they do eat up desk space. If you use PowerPoint infrequently, paper notes or print-outs can get you through a meeting. If your presentations depend on PowerPoint, find a place for a second monitor; you'll need it—and presenter view will help you track the progress of your presentations by showing you (but not the audience) what slides are coming up next.

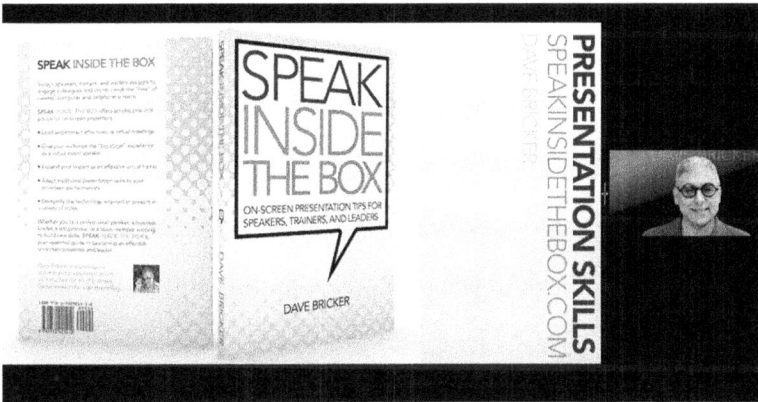

When screensharing in speaker view, your face shows up alongside your slides. Viewers can drag the center bar to adjust the relative sizes of the two images.

Don't Get Trapped in the App

Remember the monkey trap problem? Sometimes screen-sharing is less effective than other types of collaboration. You can share a word-processor screen, but why do that when you can invite others to co-edit the document with you within Google Docs? The virtual meeting is a powerful tool, but don't let it distract you. Find the best option for your needs and jump out of the meeting environment when the situation calls for it.

Stand Up; Stand Out

So far, this book has been devoted to presenting from a sitting position. You've gotten acquainted with the tools and technology you need to be an engaging participant in virtual meetings and video conversations. If you want to speak and present like a leader, it's time to prepare to leave your chair. If you're a speaker, leader, or trainer, the next chapter will help you bring the stage to the stream.

5. Create Your Virtual Stage

Capture your performance in front of a green screen, add a "big stage" background with some digital magic, and offer a video stream that makes a much bigger impression than a "talking head" on a webcam.

The equipment and technology required to set up a virtual stage are not much different or more sophisticated than your webcam and microphone setup. The principle differences are higher quality audio and video, and that a virtual stage gives presenters room to stand up and work their magic.

Why a Stage?

Keynote speakers stand up on a big stage and present to large rooms full of conference attendees. Business leaders speak to employees at corporate functions. Teachers deliver talks in large lecture halls …

Or at least they did before the coronavirus sent everyone home to work online.

Other factors threatened the speaking industry before the coronavirus showed up. Given the costs—to both corporate wallets and the environment—of putting meeting attendees on airplanes, putting them up in hotels, and putting food on their plates, virtual conferences are a smart idea. Flying speakers to a meeting destination may be worthwhile if their messages are transformational enough to offer good return on investment, but those meetings have all been canceled.

Even after we return to "business as usual," the virtual conference will have proven itself as an effective means of delighting and educating an audience. What if you could deliver a "big stage" experience to remote viewers from a home studio? How many event organizers will prefer to hire a skilled virtual presenter in a recovering economy?

Speakers who try to "wait out the hard times" will find fewer opportunities to speak live. Speakers who embrace the tools and technology they need to "stand and deliver" on-screen will get back to work faster and find more opportunities in the long run.

Whatever you think will happen to the speaking business and the meeting business, waiting for the future to turn back into the past is a risky strategy.

Too much time is wasted looking backward to watch lost opportunities sink. Those who innovate new ways to engage audiences will have the advantage. If you plan to deliver at least some of your presentations online, this chapter offers techniques you can use to return to the stage—at least virtually—and use your speaking skills to engage, enlighten, and transform audiences.

Standing Versus Sitting

Height implies social hierarchy. The tallest person in the room—the one standing—is the speaker, the leader. Stages are traditionally elevated above audience level to put the presenter "on a pedestal." We speak of "looking up to" people we admire.

Sitting is for audiences, for conversation and discussion. Sitting is for work and productivity—as long as you're not giving a presentation. If you're a gymnast, a pole vaulter, or a professional speaker, you just can't work from a chair.

Seen from a chair in front of a monitor, the faces of other meeting participants feel like they're two feet away. Using your "big" speaker voice, even to emphasize a few points, will feel unnatural and uncomfortable.

To speak with impact, get on your feet. Use your webcam for meetings; create a virtual stage for presentations. A stage gives you room to walk around and use big gestures. Standing up allows you to project and use your full vocal range. You'll do your best work in a free, open space that doesn't force you to stay "this close" to the camera, keyboard, and microphone. The difference this makes—even when you're presenting at a virtual conference table to a small group—is tremendous. "Sit at the table" using your webcam and then watch their reaction when you stand up, switch cameras, and present on your virtual stage.

Webcams are for talking; a virtual stage is for *speaking*.

Your Virtual Stage

Like real event stages, virtual stages can be small and simple or elaborate and huge. While you're free to be as grandiose and sophisticated as you can afford, this section caters to speakers on a small budget who have limited space to work in. The objective is to deliver a "big stage" experience from a spare bedroom, garage, or basement at minimal cost without having to go to film school. You will need some additional equipment and a few new skills.

The Performance Area

The typical event stage is 20–40 feet wide. A theater stage is deep enough to support big sets and a cast of actors and dancers. The conference stage varies in depth, but even a mobile stage truck offers 16 feet of room for a drum kit, lights, monitors, and guitar players and singers who swing their hair around. Big conference stages offer rear-projection or LED screens behind the speaker and off to the sides. Even if you have the space and the budget to install a full-sized stage in your home, you'll need a team of engineers to operate it for you. A smaller solution makes more sense.

If you've ever sat in the back of a conference audience, you probably spent more time watching one of the monitors on the sides of the stage than you did squinting at the tiny, distant speaker on the platform. Project this same view to your audience — zoomed in video of the speaker that captures their gestures and expressions as it follows them around the stage. This experience is easier to capture in a small home studio.

Professional speakers use the stage to "anchor" ideas. A journey from conflict to transformation may start at the right side of the

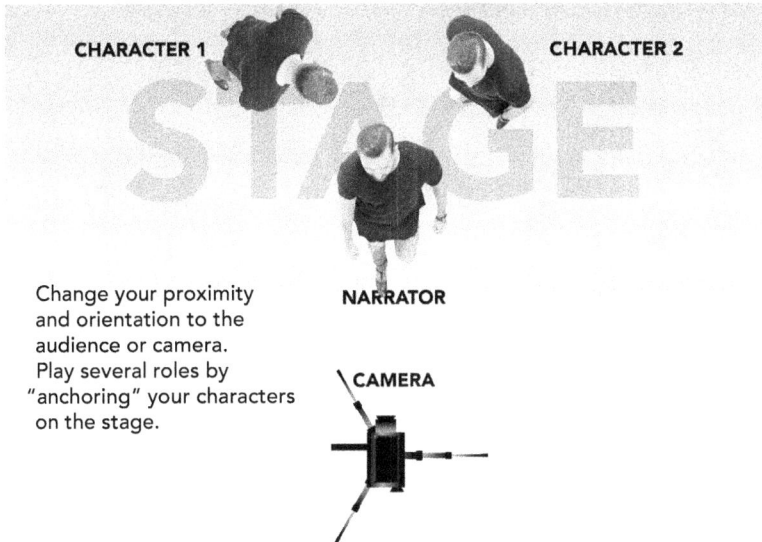

CHARACTER 1

CHARACTER 2

STAGE

NARRATOR

Change your proximity
and orientation to the
audience or camera.
Play several roles by
"anchoring" your characters
on the stage.

CAMERA

stage (the audience's left) and end up on the left (the audience's right). A speaker sharing dialogue will physically step in and out of various character roles, assuming a different role for each.

How much room do you need to work your magic on-stage? Stagecraft requires space, but a great deal of good work can be done on a 4′ x 8′ stage riser. You won't need the riser and your available space will differ from those dimensions, but experiment with giving a speech inside a taped off rectangle. Instead of "shrinking to fit" as you do in a chair, find ways to be expansive in your small performance area. Just standing up will make a dramatic difference in your performance.

Map out your performance area and set up a green screen behind it. Depending on your available space, you may wish to use a roll-down, window-shade style screen that you can retract when you're not filming.

The Green Screen

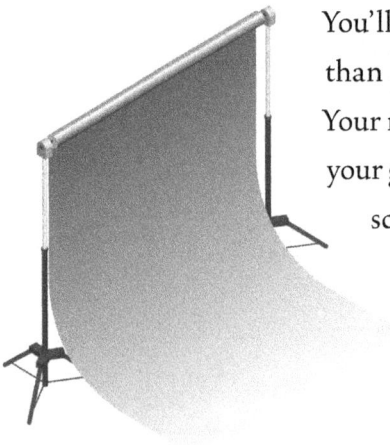

You'll need a larger green screen for a virtual stage than you will for a webcam focused on a chair. Your range of motion will be limited by the size of your green screen and how close you can get to the screen without casting shadows on it. Get the largest chromakey screen you can fit behind your performance area, and set it up as far behind you as you reasonably can. Perform more than four feet away from the screen for better results.

Instead of a fabric screen, consider purchasing a roll of heavy chromakey paper that can be mounted on the wall or ceiling. Pull it down like a window shade and retract it with a chain loop. Paper doesn't wrinkle easily like fabric, and retracting the screen when it's not in use will keep it in better condition. An added benefit is that your home office won't have a giant green rectangle hanging in it when you're not filming.

Softbox light

A set of "softbox" lights aimed at the green screen behind your presentation area will keep the screen evenly lit.

As mentioned before, the art of green screen videography is a vast subject. Consult the YouTube oracle for advice on lights, filming in small spaces, and other details. You'll find many experts willing to share their knowledge, experience, and successful trial-and-error experiments.

Video Cameras

Your webcam is not an ideal tool for shooting performance video. It has a tiny lens and a small sensor.

Add a quality video camera or DSLR[5] to your setup. Phone cameras have improved, but a proper video camera has a larger

5. DSLR — A Digital Single Lens Reflex camera looks and functions like a traditional film camera, but its high-quality lens and image sensor can capture video.

DSLR and camcorder

and higher quality lens and better low-light adjustment features. The better the camera, the better your video quality will be.

A 4K camera has twice the resolution of a standard HD (1080p) video camera. That means you'll capture more detail for live streaming and recording. Even if your final video output is HD, you'll be able to zoom in up to 200% without losing quality.

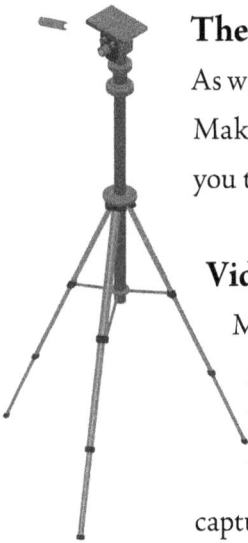

The Tripod

As with a webcam, your camera should be positioned at face level. Make sure your tripod is tall enough (and stable enough) to give you the angle you need.

Video Capture

Most computers are not equipped to receive a live video feed from a camcorder. You'll need a camera that offers "clean HDMI" output (a video image that's free of camera menus, battery status, and other visual data) and an added video capture card or converter. Run a cable from your camera's HDMI output port into the video capture converter. Small converters plug into one of your computer's USB3 ports. More sophisticated video capture cards require an open PCIE slot on your PC or MacPro.

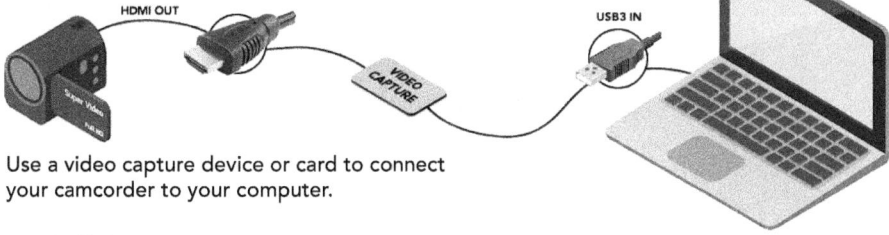

Use a video capture device or card to connect your camcorder to your computer.

If all these acronyms (HD, 4K, HDMI, DSLR, USB3, etc.) are disconcerting, be reassured that we've now covered most of the ones you'll need to know. See the Appendix for a list of common terms and acronyms.

Once your video camera is connected to a capture card or device, it will appear in the list of cameras available to your computer operating system and meeting software. To switch from your webcam to your video camera, open the preferences and select it from the menu.

A number of budget 4K "web streaming" camcorders offer direct to USB3 video. At the time of this writing, the major camera manufacturers (Sony, Nikon, Canon, et al) have not followed suit, but they likely will. Check specs and options, and read reviews carefully before buying an off-brand or "knock-off" camera.

Video Switches

Video switches offer an alternative to selecting a camera within the "choose camera" menu in the settings/preferences panel of your meeting software. A desktop video switch allows you to plug in two or more cameras, and the switch is plugged into your video capture system. Click a button to change cameras. This is faster than opening up computer windows and changing preferences. If you decide to livestream a virtual presentation with, for example, a full-view camera and a close-up camera, a helper can use the switch to instantly cut from one camera to another, much as a video engineer would when controlling the big screen displays at the sides of an event stage.

Video switches range in price and features, but a simple one can be purchased for under $30.

Microphones

What microphone do you use for live presentations? Lavalier and headset mics are most common; they free you to gesture with their hands and they stay the same distance from your mouth as you move about the stage.

Use whatever microphone you're most comfortable with. Wireless systems reduce "cable spaghetti" but a few twist ties and neat storage habits can make any system work.

As with any other gear, the higher the quality, the better the result. A directional microphone aimed at your mouth is less likely to pick up sounds from the room and surrounding environment. An omnidirectional microphone will pick up more sounds that weren't made by you. Why risk picking up the barking dogs, the yard man, the passing fire truck, and the output from your speakers when simple technology will keep viewers' ears focused on you?

Monitors

When speaking to an audience, feedback is important. Reading faces enables you to know your participants are laughing at your jokes, nodding to affirm your powerful truths, and not yawning.

In a live audience presentation, making eye contact with a crowded room requires a lot of technique. In a virtual presentation, the camera lets you look every viewer in the eye—as long as you look into the camera.

Place a large monitor directly behind the camera that displays your meeting attendees in gallery view. If the monitor is off to the side, that voice in your head that constantly asks, "How am I doing?" will have you looking away to check. Even if the audience monitor is partially blocked by the camera, you'll see enough of their faces and reactions to pace and adjust your presentation without diverting your attention from the lens.

In most cases, this requires a second monitor that displays the meeting running on your desktop.

An audience monitor helps you speak directly to meeting attendees without having to look elsewhere for feedback.

Teleprompters

Do you need a teleprompter? Most professional speakers present without notes, and very few of them read their speeches from a script (though the great orator, Winston Churchill read all of his). If you're familiar with your material, you won't need anything more than an outline to "stay on the rails," but when introducing a chapter in an online course or creating "one-off" content, a teleprompter can be helpful. A portable teleprompter can be purchased for under $250.

The teleprompter places the video camera behind an angled pane of glass. In front of the glass, a tablet or phone displays and scrolls your text in reverse so its reflection can be read. The reflected text is too close to the lens for the camera to see, so it won't appear on the final video. The camera films you through your text so you'll be looking right at the lens as you read.

Getting content from your computer to your tablet and setting it up in the teleprompter app is a minor hassle. Use a teleprompter only if your content demands it.

As an alternative, outlines and short scripts can be printed on one or two sheets of paper in print large enough to read from where you're presenting. Tie some paper clips to some thread, clip them to the papers, and tape the thread to the ceiling so your papers hang next to the camera lens. Add more paper clips at the bottoms of the paper to serve as weights if the air-conditioner blows them around. From four or five feet away from the camera, a glance at the text a few inches off to one side of the camera won't be noticeable in the final video.

The Digital Background

All the tools and technology in the world won't make much of an impression if your presentation background doesn't deliver a "big stage" experience. The camera and green screen—all that "beyond the webcam" stuff was all done in favor of making you look great in front of something digital.

Whether that environment is a classroom, a conference room, or an event stage, think about what a camera view of you working in that space would look like.

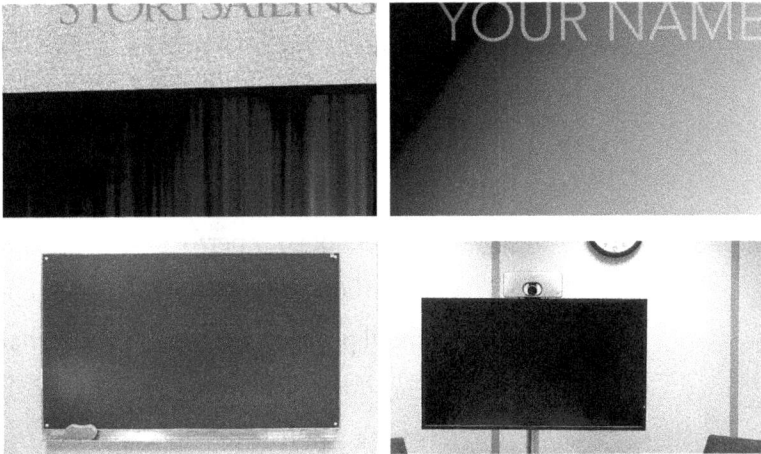

Digital backgrounds:
Upper left: a piece of the "big stage"
Upper right: a simple background texture with your name or brand
Lower left: classroom
Lower right: conference room

Are you standing next to a whiteboard at the front of the classroom or conference table?

Picture the typical large event stage. Perhaps there's a big LED screen behind you and above your head. Usually a central screen is used for branding, but doesn't feature a lot of motion that distracts eyes from the speaker. Perhaps the very bottom of your logo is visible behind your head. This "window into a larger world" suggests that the setting is much bigger than the camera frame. Are there red curtains? Banners with the name of the conference on them?

Is the camera shooting you and your background perfectly centered and aligned with the stage? In the real world, probably not. Consider a slightly off-center, angled view that introduces natural, human imperfection.

Be sure not to include objects in your image that create scale conflicts. The big stage will look authentic unless there's a picture of a lectern in it that appears to be twice the height of the speaker.

The creation of your background image is not a DIY job for the average professional who has no design training. Talk to a graphic designer about your goals when you work on critical piece of your performance. Designing a great background or even a small collection of them is a small project for a capable artist that will make the difference between looking amateur and delivering a polished "big stage" experience.

Stand and Deliver!

You're almost ready to start presenting. With your camera and microphone connected to your computer, open a one-person session in your meeting software. Open the settings/preferences panel (or use your fancy switching gear) and make sure you are able to access your camcorder and microphone.

Zoom your camera out and then slowly zoom in until the green screen completely fills the frame. Anything that isn't green will show up on your video as the actual background in your office as seen through a hole in the edge of your digital background. Move your camera and screen as far apart as possible to maximize your range. My studio is narrow, so I installed a camera wall-mount opposite the chromakey screen at the desired height. This gives me an additional foot of distance, eliminates the tripod and the space it uses in my small studio, and keeps my camera cables close to the wall and out of the way.

Practice working in your performance area as you watch yourself on-screen.

Some camera monitors and most meeting software give you an option to "mirror my image." When filming yourself, if you move to your right, you may see yourself move to the left on the camera monitor. Remember, your right is the audience's left; the camera sees what the audience will see. In "mirror mode," if you move to the right, your image will move to the right—as if you were watching yourself in a mirror. Though technically backward, it's a lot more comfortable and intuitive to work with. "Mirror mode" won't change what the audience sees on the final video; it's just there to help you while performing.

Left: It can be disconcerting to move to the right and watch yourself move to the left in the monitor.

Right: Switch "mirror my image" on to have the monitor mimic what you'd see in a mirror.

Move from left to right and get a feel for how wide the virtual stage is. How big was that fish? Where can you begin the journey from conflict to transformation and where does it end on the other side of the stage?

Move toward the camera. As you get closer, you'll reach a point where the top of your head gets cropped out of the scene. Adjust the camera angle as needed.

Move back toward the green screen. How much of your body can you fit in the shot? [6] A presentation given from the waist up can still be very effective.

Keep experimenting with your proximity to the camera. Adjust the camera angle to maximize the effective range from distant to close-up shooting. With some trial and error, you'll be able to get close to the camera without cropping off the top of your head and still get a good body shot.

The goal is to be able to set your camera up before you shoot so you won't need anyone to operate it for you during your performance. With some practice, you'll learn to move toward and away from the camera during your performance. Fill the frame with your head and shoulders to emphasize a point or back away to show more gestures, anchor points on a timeline or journey, or play characters in a dialogue.

6. If you have room to shoot your whole body, you may want to extend your green screen down under your feet or paint a piece of plywood with green chromakey paint to serve as an invisible floor.

6. The Virtual Trainer

Unlike keynote speakers who usually spend the entire session addressing the audience from the stage, teachers and trainers must shift between lecturing and interactive activities. There's gray area here, too, because while it's easy to speak next to a PowerPoint presentation and advance the slides with a remote control, some interactive exercises require that the trainer have access to a keyboard, mouse, and other online tools.

One way to accomplish this is by adding a lectern with a laptop to the performance area, but this adds clutter to an already-small stage, and requires a certain amount of fancy signal switching when the presenter wishes to change from "speaker view" to "training screen view."

If you're fortunate enough to have an assistant available to adjust your video feeds, quick switching gets easier, but a system you can operate yourself has clear advantages.

As you reconfigure your training sessions to work in a virtual environment, map out what kinds of content you need to appear on the screen for each section of the session. An introduction or conclusion might be well-suited to the virtual stage view. This "keynote view" also works well alongside a PowerPoint presentation in a split window, though you will need to get to your desktop to enter screensharing mode. If you want to use the variety of interactive training tools—whiteboards, graphing and charting applications, polls and quizzes, etc.—it may make sense to switch to your webcam and chair. From your desk, you'll be better able to mute and un-mute participants, break "virtual tables" into separate breakout rooms, and interact with individual participants.

Too much moving back and forth between your desktop and your virtual stage is a distraction. Choreograph your session so trainees see the most appropriate views of you and your content at any given time.

Interactivity

The secret to engaging an audience—especially if your material is dry or technical—is interactivity of the personal, not the digital kind. Ask questions. Involve attendees in group exercises. Divide the room into teams. Keep the discussion going. If they're not laughing, they're not learning.

Interactivity can be more difficult when you can't call people up on stage or walk out among your attendees, but online meeting platforms offer advantages, too. As on-screen training tools have become more sophisticated, live trainers have been relying on them more and more at live sessions.

Learn the full suite of tools available in a variety of meeting platforms. As you learn about polls and whiteboards and breakout rooms, ask yourself, "How can I use that feature?" "Which of my cameras is best suited to working with that tool?" "How can I use this feature to connect attendees around my ideas and help them share their thoughts, experiences, conclusions, and questions with the group? The more you bring your attendees on-screen to interact with you and each other around your content, the more effective your training will be.

Change the Subject?

The title and subject of your training may be another monkey trap. Is your content as relevant to an online audience as it was to a live one? You may need to let go of old ideas if they don't work in the virtual training room.

Before the coronavirus lockdown, I gave workshops on presentation skills. Now that live presentation skills are in decreased

Technology changes fast. We all have to keep up.

demand, I have switched to teaching virtual presentation skills (hence, this book). Few of my trainees have a virtual stage so when we discuss using the stage to anchor timelines and characters, I suggest equivalent hand gestures and how to adjust their proximity to the camera. Topics like camera, mic, and keyboard positions; green screens; and lights never came up in my live sessions, but these ideas are important and relevant to my online trainees' success.

Adapt, adopt, and trim the dead branches. Redevelop your content to fit the delivery medium and maximize your on-screen presence. Look good, sound good, and deliver the "big stage" or "big classroom" experience, even when "speaking inside the box."

7. Expand Your On-Screen Presence

Thus far, the strategies suggested in this book were designed to be set up and implemented by one person. With some additional technology and professional support, you can accomplish even more. Here are options to consider:

Live or Recorded?

Feeding live video into an online meeting brings the "tightrope factor"—the spontaneity to react to the moment, interact with guests, and deal with technical problems in front of an audience. Live performance also carries the stammers, stutters, coughs, and perhaps even a few things you wish you hadn't said. It introduces camera switching challenges that a live speaker would never have to deal with.

Prerecording a presentation will kill some of the spontaneity, but without the pressure of realtime broadcasting, much magic can be accomplished in the editing room. Aside from cutting and splicing to fix less-than-stellar material, the camera can cut between wide and tight shots and screensharing. You can introduce footage shot on different cameras at different angles. The possibilities for color correction and special effects are endless — as long as you have a capable engineer to assist.

If you're shooting for an online course or webinar, advance recording will give you the best possible output. If you're live-streaming for an event, the organizers may want you "there" to respond to questions, engage remote participants, and reference events of the day.

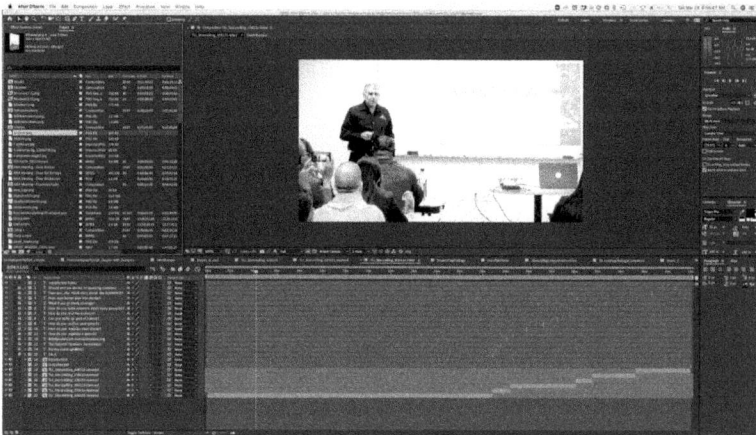

Video editing software allows you to do remarkable things with recorded video.

When hired as a virtual speaker, discuss the pros and cons of live and recorded performance with the meeting organizer. If the meeting host wants to license your content to distribute as a webinar to employees who can't attend the initial broadcast, it may make more sense to record and edit a perfect session for them.

Multiple Cameras

With enough inputs on your video capture interface, you can easily set up two or more cameras on your virtual stage. Each camera can produce a close-up shot, a full-body shot, or some angle. Robotic motion-tracking cameras will stay focused on your face so you won't have to worry about moving out of the view of the close-up camera.

Artful switching between cameras during a live performance is something you'll need an assistant to help with. Or you can step up to a timed, automatic switching system.

With a recorded session, it's much easier to combine footage from different cameras, or even use two levels of magnification from the same camera.

Switch between multiple cameras to stream different views on the fly.

Learn to edit your own videos or share your files with a remote video editor. Bear in mind that video editing requires a fast computer with lots of memory and storage space. If you'd rather focus on presentation, get good at capturing high quality footage and find a videographer partner to assemble the final product.

The 3D Event Stage

Another step up is to have a 3D artist create a model of a real event stage with lights, big screens, steps with neon lights, and anything else you'd see at an elaborate event. This model can be pulled into the video-editing software, rendered in photorealism, and through the magic of the green screen, you'll be seen on the "Ginormous stage." Need a stadium full of screaming fans? Searchlights? Fog effects with lasers? It can all be done in 3D.

3D model of an event stage. After editing, the middle screen can show the event name and logo, and the outside screens can show a multicamera view of the presenter.

A 3D event stage is very difficult to use for a live, streaming performance and nearly impossible to pull off on your own. The tools are expensive and sophisticated. And at some point, the speaker gets upstaged ... by the stage! This "Hollywood" approach may make sense for a celebrity speaker, but it's overkill for the typical speaker, business leader, or trainer.

Those attracted to this type of presentation will be better served to take the advice in the following section.

Build a Real Stage

If you have budget and space and available — for example, an empty garage — consider building a stage set with a raised performance area, a backdrop, curtains, and lights. Instead of shooting with a green screen, shoot on an actual physical stage. Once the lights and camera positions are worked out, leave everything in-place and ready to switch on. You can even add vertical banners at the sides of the stage and paint them with green chromakey paint. When editing, drop in custom video or graphics to replace the green areas.

Work with a TV studio

If you need to go beyond the home studio virtual stage or just don't want to set up cameras and microphones and screens and lights, contact your local television studio. Television studios have the green screen rooms, lights, high-end cameras, streaming equipment, and (most important) the

talented artists and engineers you need to pull off a big production or even a quality small one. Once you've established your requirements and had any virtual scenery created, your studio should be able to pull up your files, set you up on the green screen stage with professional lighting and quickly shoot a beautiful, virtual performance for streaming or post-production editing.

If you have access to a studio, plan to spend accordingly. Good talent and high-end equipment are an investment.

8. Performance Tips

Love Means Never Having to Say You're Sorry

Audiences want you to fix their problems, not listen to you gripe about yours. Technological glitches and human error are inevitable, just as they are on a real stage. Don't make excuses or offer apologies. When you forget to unmute yourself or share your screen and then have to start up your PowerPoint presentation, fix or bypass the problem and move forward as smoothly as possible. Your viewers are learning to manage their own on-screen tools. They understand the challenges and will be motivated by speakers who handle technology with humor and grace.

Practice "Social Distancing"

The presence of meeting attendees' faces on a monitor two feet from your face will trigger your instincts to hold back and quiet down. Remind yourself that it's okay to use your full speaking range—from high to low, loud to soft, and mild to wild. Get out of "conversation mode" and switch into "speaker mode." Your presentation will be much more dynamic and engaging, even if you're in a chair.

Anchor Important Points

On the stage, speakers use different positions on the stage to "anchor" narrative journeys through time and progress. A speaker might start a talk about the old, hard times on the right side of the stage (the audience's left) and proceed across the platform as the story moves toward transformation. When sharing dialogue, a speaker might move forward to narrate and then step back and to deliver lines as the characters in the story. By switching sides, the dialogue is "acted out" and the need for past tense dialogue tags (I said, "_____." Then Bill said, "_____.") is eliminated. The audience sees the interaction happen in present-tense real time.

If presenting on a virtual stage, you probably have room to anchor points and characters in the traditional way. If presenting in a chair, use an office chair with wheels. Pivoting the chair slightly will produce the desired shift of your image from one side of the screen to the other.

Slide a few feet away from the screen to give yourself more working room. A short increase in distance makes a dramatic difference in how much of you the audience can see, and you'll feel less inhibited about speaking up.

Look Sharp! You Never Know Who's in the Room

Stories abound of speakers who were surprised to find that their presentation was viewed by an influencer who later hired them. Don't get lazy about your on-screen appearance, even if it's your tenth webinar of the week. Setting up lights, cameras, green screens, and digital backgrounds is more work, but it's work that will help you stand out. Let all those other speakers try to engage audiences while backlit by their wall sconces or showing off their office clutter. One person noticing the difference in your presentation standards can change your fortunes. You wouldn't speak on a stage with shabby clothes or an ungroomed hair. Treat every on-screen appearance as an audition, an opportunity to show off your commitment to delivering value to your audience.

Throw Your Window Out the Window

Lighting deserves one more mention. Sunlight streaming through windows is the most common cause of backlit, high-contrast, poor quality images. Even if the window isn't behind you, the intensity of the light will vary through the day, making it difficult to adjust your lighting. One hour you're a shadow with a white background; the next, you're a pale ghost with "hot spot" highlights. When presenting, draw the shades and control your lighting with predictable sources of illumination.

9. Speak Inside the Box: Conclusion

Speaking "inside the box" requires new skills, technology, and equipment. Push yourself to master the basics of video production. When you see yourself "up on the big stage," you'll smile. If they only knew what my studio really looked like!

Though the webcam-microphone-keyboard combination in the average laptop is convenient, professional presenters gain the advantage by uncoupling these components. It may seem like an unnecessary expense to add lights, a chromakey screen, and a custom background to your day-to-day videoconferencing tools, but a proper set-up costs less than a decent office chair or a pair of fashionable shoes. Invest in your on-screen appearance. "Good enough" just isn't good enough for those who want to stand out in a work-at-home world. It's so easy to look sharp at the digital conference table. Why wouldn't you if it's that easy?

Professional speakers get hired to deliver a "big stage" experience. "Talking heads" fall short. When it's time to present, get on your feet. Standing expands your vocal range, gives you a stage to walk, and allows you to put your hands and body to work. A high-quality camera will improve the color and contrast of your video feed. All of these translate into benefits for you audience.

If you're wondering what webcam to buy, how big a green screen to set up, which microphone you need, and whether or not you can use your existing camcorder, the answers to your questions are constantly changing. New tools and technology are being released all the time. Online meeting platforms are evolving like crazy.

Now that you understand the parts and pieces of a home video studio and the value each provides, resist the urge to go shopping. Watch some YouTube tutorials on green screens. Learn about different types of microphones. Read reviews on the latest webcams. If you need to, reach out to a video producer and hire them to help you put a system together.

Start off with your desktop webcam and get comfortable working with a green screen, lights, and a digital background. If you're a trainer, familiarize yourself with the range of new tools available and rework your live programs to engage viewers online. Once your desktop tools become familiar, the virtual stage will be a simple addition.

Whether you share your message live or on-screen, people will always need inspiration, engagement, and interaction. If this book helps you use your speaking skill to change minds and fortunes, it will have served a noble purpose.

—Dave Bricker

About the Author

Dave Bricker is a professional speaker, business storyteller, and presentation coach. He's an advanced Toastmaster and a member of the National Speakers Association. Dave is an award-winning author of numerous books, has an MFA in Graphic Design, and spent years of his life solo adventure sailing on a small boat.

Learn more about Dave Bricker's live and remote speaking and workshop programs and subscribe to the StorySailing® newsletter at www.StorySailing.com

Keep up with the world of Virtualoso Presentation skills at www.speakinsidethebox.com

Appendix: Common Terms and Acronyms

4K Video is twice the resolution (3840 pixels wide x 2160 pixels tall) of HD

DSLR – A Single Lens Reflex Camera looks like a traditional 35mm film camera. Digital SLRs use a sensor instead of film, and today's models can also shoot video. Some videographers take advantage of the DSLR's high-quality sensor and wide assortment of available lenses.

HD – High Definition video is also known as 1080p video. The actual signal is 1920 pixels wide by 1080 pixels tall.

HDMI (High Definition Multimedia Interface) is a standard port on most cameras, computers, and multimedia projectors. As a speaker, you may have run into a projector that required you to convert from your HDMI signal to an older VGA-style interface.

Pixel – A digital image (still or video) is made up of a grid of tiny, colored squares. These individual squares are "pixels." The number of pixels that define the height and width of an image are its "resolution."

USB (**Universal Serial Bus**) has been a standard computer connection port for a long time. Though the familiar rectangular plugs on flash keys, keyboards, etc. haven't changed, USB has been released in faster and faster versions (USB2 and USB3). USB3 replaced Firewire, which was the high-speed standard for a while.

VGA (**Video Graphics Array**) is an old standard that only supports 640 pixels wide x 480 pixels tall images. The HD standard not only went to higher resolution, it changed the old 4:3 screen ratio (width to height) to a new "widescreen" 16:9 ratio. You'll need a separate audio cable if using VGA.

XLR (**External Line Return**) connector—a standard 3-contact microphone connector.

Image Credits

USB plug - https://www.vecteezy.com/free-vector/hdmi

Ethernet - https://www.vecteezy.com/free-vector/ethernet

Tripod / Videographer - https://www.freepik.com/free-photos-vectors/character, Character vector created by macrovector - www.freepik.com

Lights and screen - https://www.freepik.com/free-photos-vectors/background, Background vector created by macrovector - www.freepik.com

Speakers - https://www.freepik.com/free-photos-vectors/banner, Banner vector created by macrovector - www.freepik.com

Microphones - https://www.freepik.com/free-photos-vectors/music, Music vector created by macrovector - www.freepik.com

DSLR - https://www.vecteezy.com/free-vector/realistic-dslr-camera

Office Desk - "https://www.freepik.com/free-photos-vectors/computer, Computer vector created by macrovector - www.freepik.com

Camera on tripod - https://www.vecteezy.com/free-vector/tripod

Studio Lights - https://www.freepik.com/free-photos-vectors/technology, Technology vector created by freepik - www.freepik.com

Camcorder - https://www.freepik.com/free-photos-vectors/card, Card vector created by macrovector - www.freepik.com

Computer - https://www.freepik.com/free-photos-vectors/music, Music vector created by sentavio - www.freepik.com

https://commons.wikimedia.org/wiki/File:Katherine_Maher-2.jpg • VGrigas, background removed by User: Eatcha • This file is licensed under the Creative Commons Attribution-Share Alike 3.0 Unported license

Images of meeting participants used with permission

All other images licensed, adapted from product photos, or created by the author.

Because independent writers and publishers should be held to the same high standards as the mainstream publishing industry, I encourage you to post an honest and objective review of this book on Amazon.com or the online bookstore of your choice.

Thank you,

— Dave Bricker